EGMONT
We bring stories to life

First published in Great Britain 2019 by Egmont UK Limited
The Yellow Building, 1 Nicholas Road, London W11 4AN

Illustrations by Gregory Sokol
Written by Katrina Pallant
Designed by Maddox Philpot

© & ™ 2019 Lucasfilm Ltd.
ISBN 978 1 4052 9337 2
70303/001
Printed in UK

To find more great *Star Wars* books, visit
www.egmont.co.uk/starwars

STAR WARS

MINI MAZES

Join the Rebellion, meet your
favourite characters and defeat
the First Order in this awesome
maze book!

Use your Jedi skills to complete
each maze from start to finish.
Watch out for obstacles and danger
along the way.

Some mazes are trickier than
others. If you get stuck, there are
answers at the back of the book.

Naboo royalty wear elaborate robes. find your way across Padmé's dress.

Start

Finish

Start —

C-3PO's circuits are exposed. Make sure he's in working order.

Finish

The seas of Naboo are filled with opee sea killers. Which one has caught the submarine?

Start

Finish

Follow the path of the Sith
across Darth Maul's face.

Coruscant welcomes citizens from all over the galaxy.
Can you find your way around the city?

Start

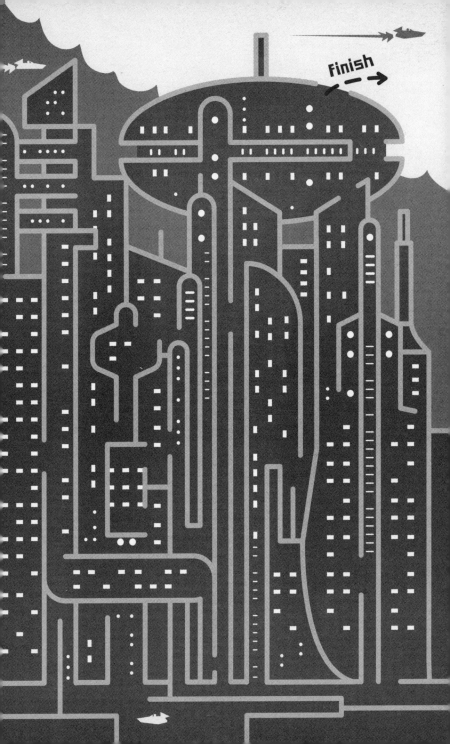

finish → →

Finish

Start

The attack on the Trade
Federation ship is underway.
Help the Naboo pilots destroy
the control ship!

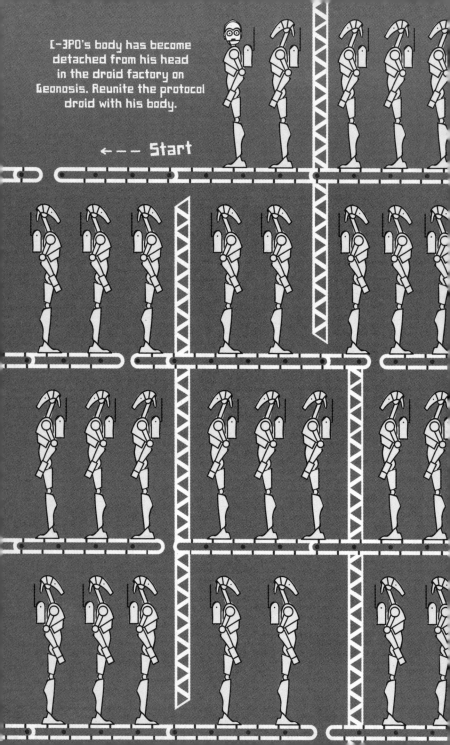

C-3PO's body has become detached from his head in the droid factory on Geonosis. Reunite the protocol droid with his body.

← – – Start

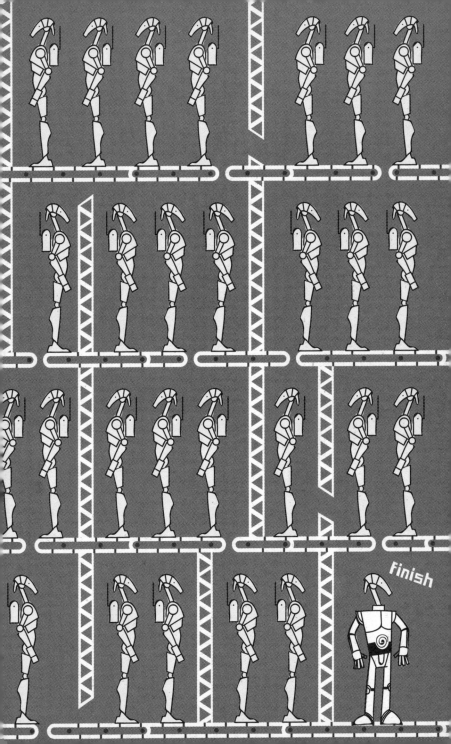

Finish

Obi-Wan Kenobi has an important message. Navigate through the holocron.

Finish

Start

Chewbacca is ready to fight.
Be careful not to get caught
in the crosshairs!
Start
Finish

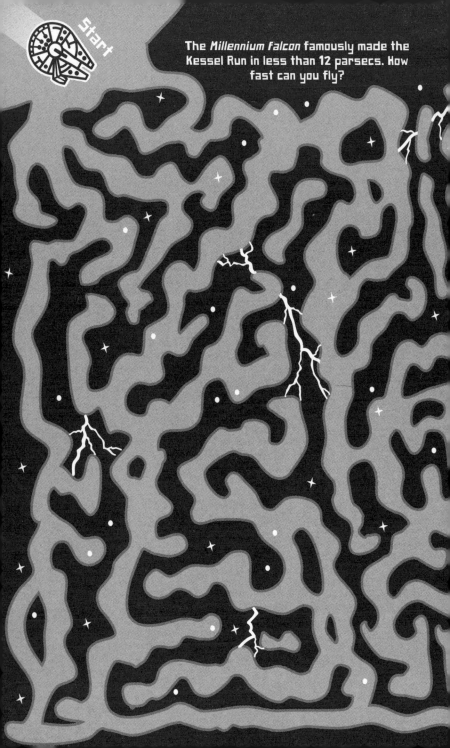

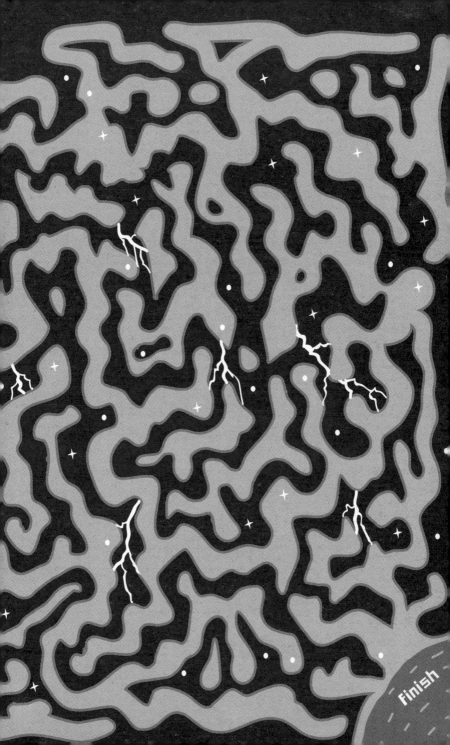

finish

The rebels prepare their attack on the Scarif Imperial base. Help them through the shield gate.

finish

Start

The scaly dewback is great for transport through the hot desert. Travel from its head to its tail.

finish

Start

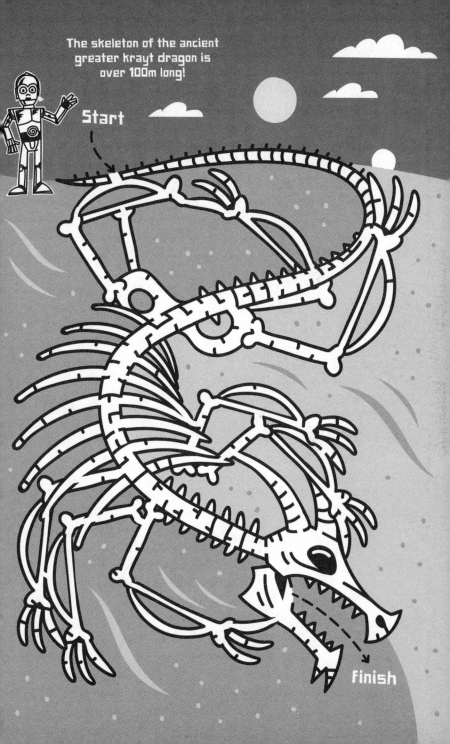

The skeleton of the ancient greater krayt dragon is over 100m long!

Start

Finish

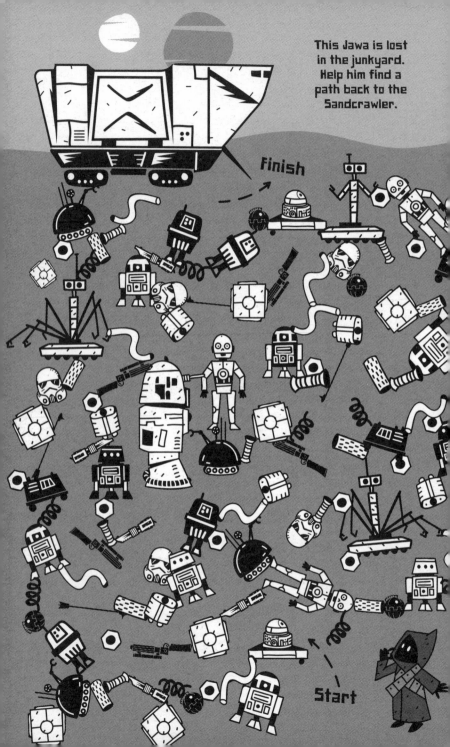

This Jawa is lost in the junkyard. Help him find a path back to the Sandcrawler.

Finish

Start

Greedo is a grumpy bounty hunter. Watch out for his quick draw!

finish

Start

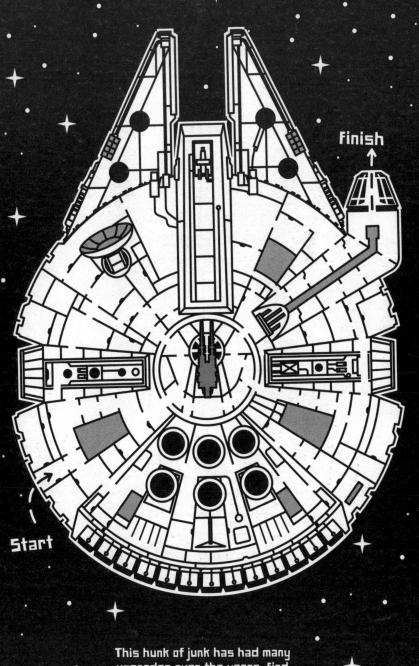

Finish

Start

This hunk of junk has had many
upgrades over the years. Find
you way across the *Falcon*.

R2-D2 is messing with Imperial computers to help his friends out of a tough situation. Give him a hand by navigating the circuit board.

Finish →

Start

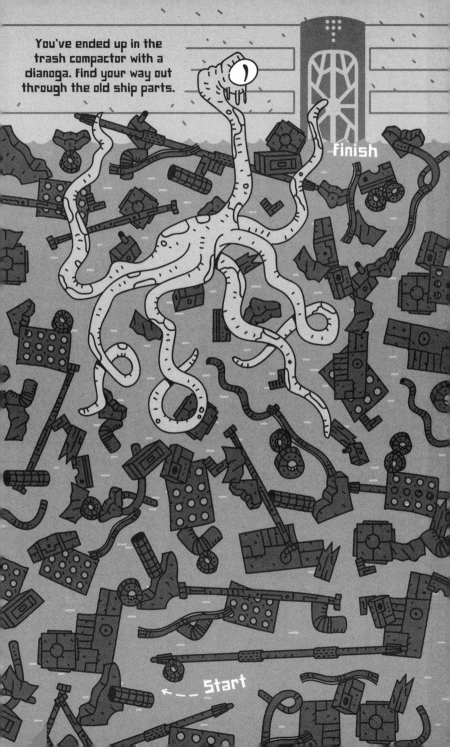

Finish

Start

The Death Star is a busy place. Help the mouse droid get to its destination.

Finish

Start

The Death Star is
fully operational.
Time to make
your move!

Time to destroy the Death Star! Complete the trench run for victory.

finish

Start

finish

Start

BOOM! The Rebel Alliance has destroyed
the Empire's superweapon. Fly away from
the exploding Death Star.

← – – – Start

Run through the snowy plains of Hoth to escape the hungry wampa.

Finish ←

Start

Start

Asteroids ahead!
Dodge the space
debris to escape
the TIE fighters.

finish

Finish

Sometimes, when you land in a cave in space, it turns out to be the mouth of a terrifying exogorth!

Start

Finish

Start

Luke has arrived on Dagobah to
continue his Jedi training. Help him
find the old Jedi master, Yoda.

Soar through the air to reach the floating Cloud City above Bespin.

Finish

Start

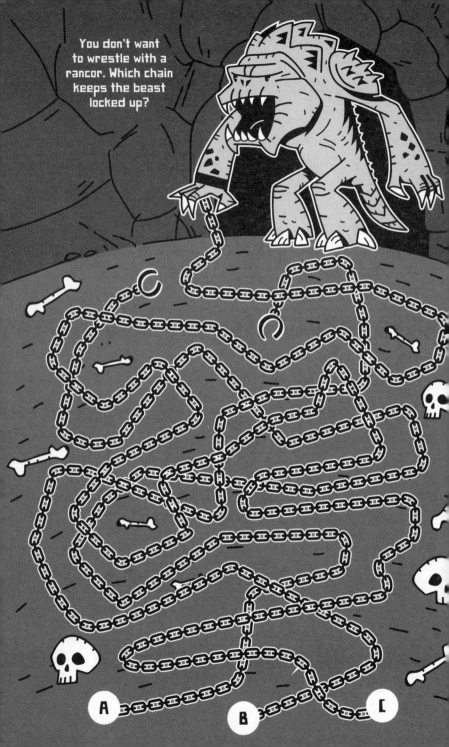

finish

Start

Boba Fett's jet pack sends
him soaring in the sky –
handy for a quick exit!

Boba Fett flew too close to the sarlacc pit! Which tentacle leads to the famous bounty hunter?

Bright Tree Village can be difficult to navigate for non-Ewoks. Use the swing bridges to get to the finish.

Start

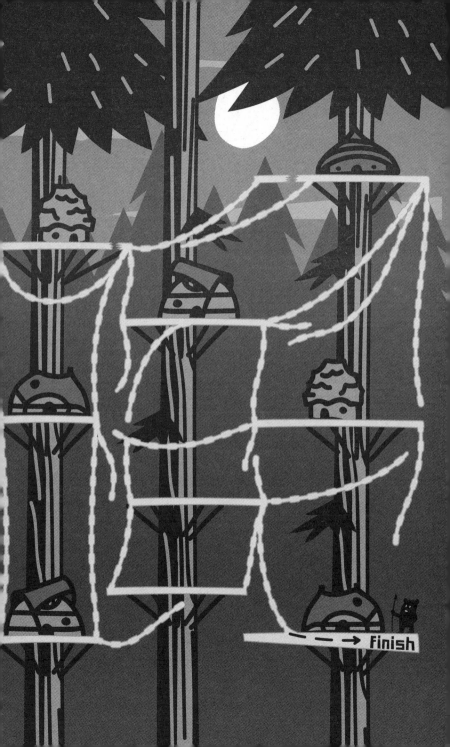

finish

Uh oh! The Emperor has unleashed his Force-lightning. Work out how to escape his wrath.

Start

Finish

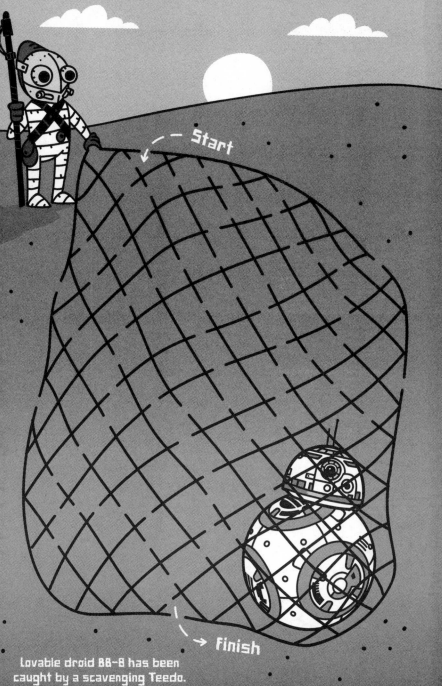

Start

Finish

Lovable droid BB-8 has been
caught by a scavenging Teedo.
Help him out of the net.

Finn needs a drink of water. Be careful not to upset the mighty happabore!

Finish

Start

Finish

Follow the *Falcon* over
the Star Destroyer to
escape the First Order.

Start

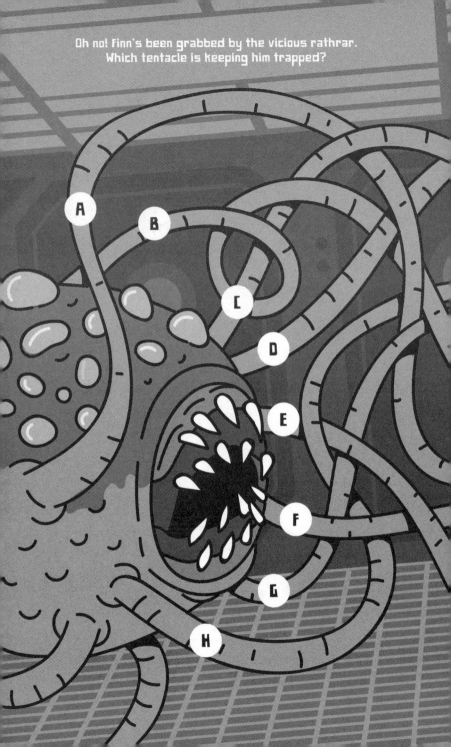

Finish

Start ←--

It's a battle for good versus evil!
Can you find your way out in one piece?

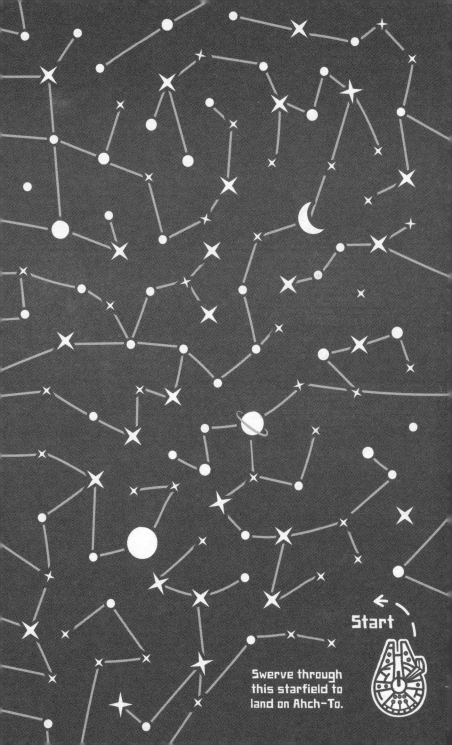

Start

Swerve through
this starfield to
land on Ahch-To.

Start

Porgs everywhere!
find your way
through these
cute creatures.

finish

Start

Finish

BB-8 is rolling away from the First Order. Help
the loyal little droid by completing the maze.

Finish

Start —

The galaxy's elite come to Canto Bight for a good time. Make your way around the games table.

Solutions

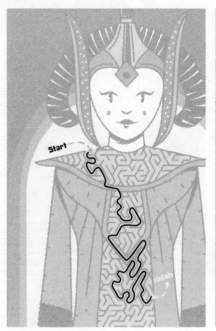

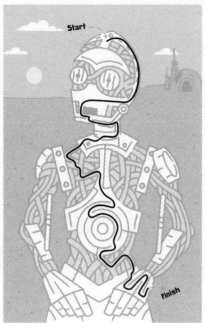

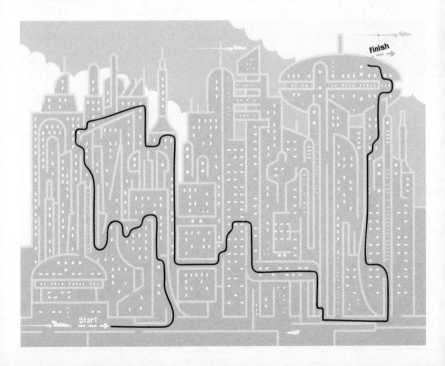

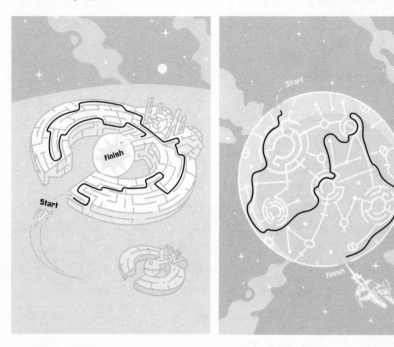

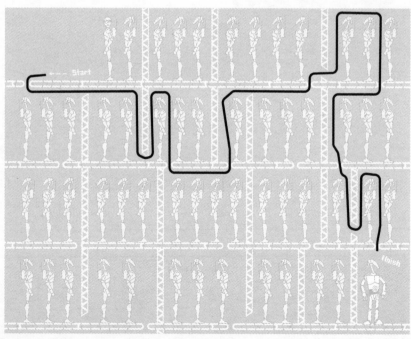

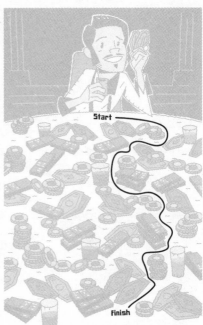

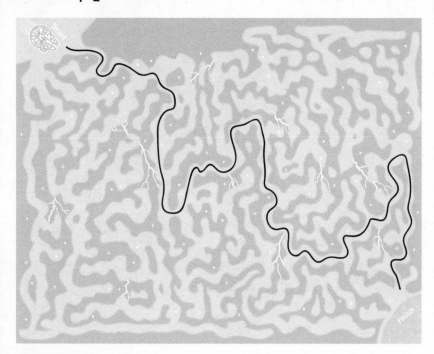

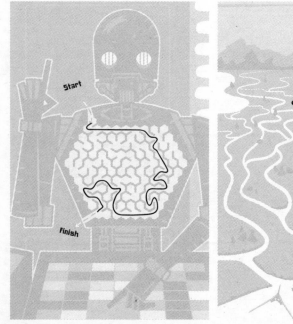

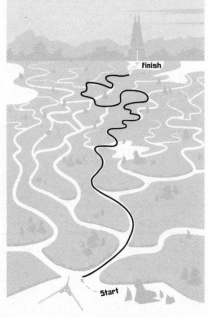

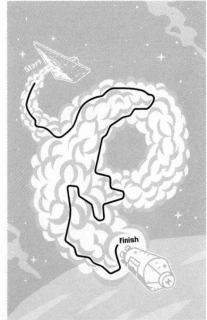

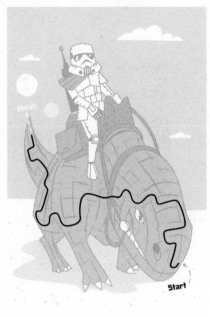

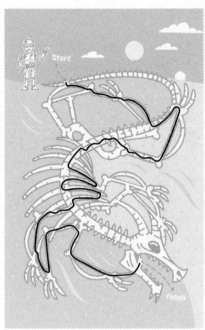

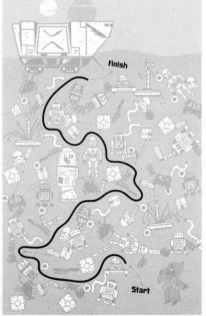

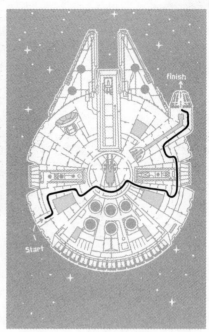
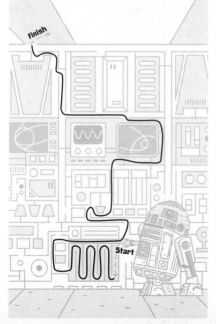
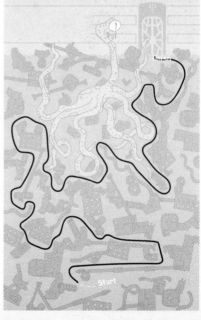

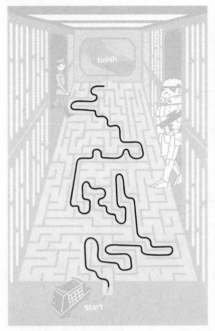

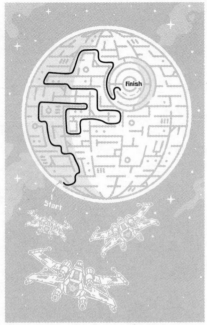

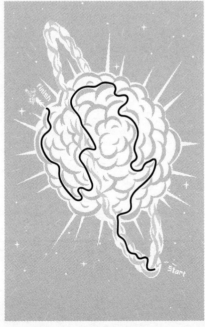

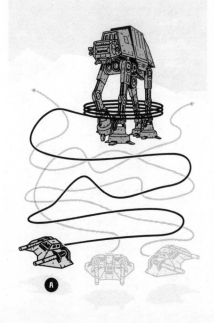

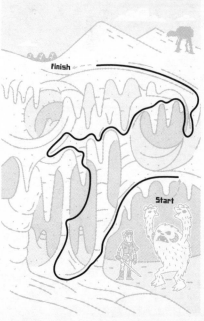

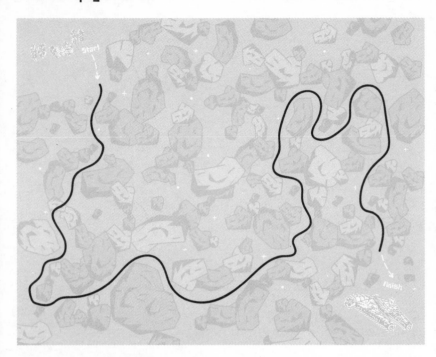

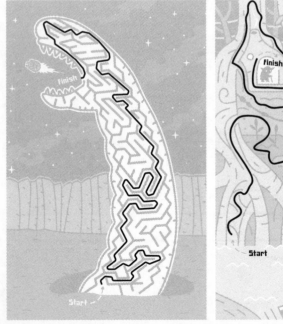

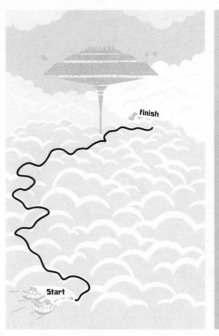

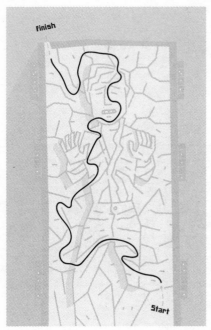

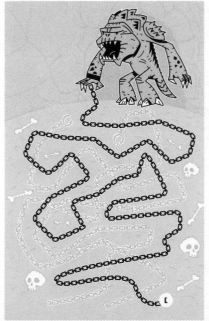

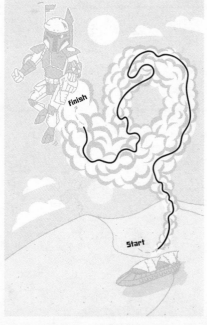

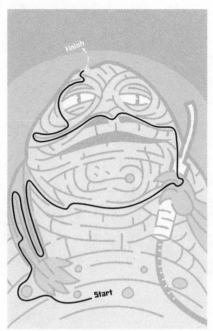

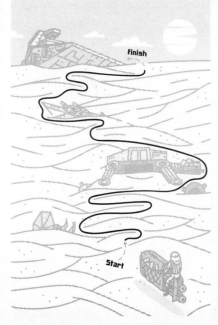

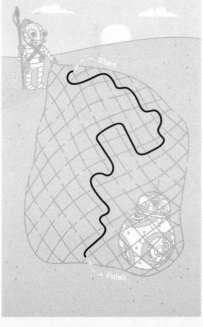

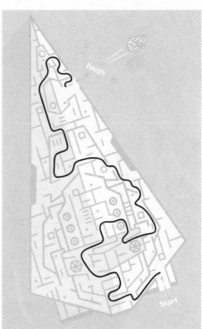

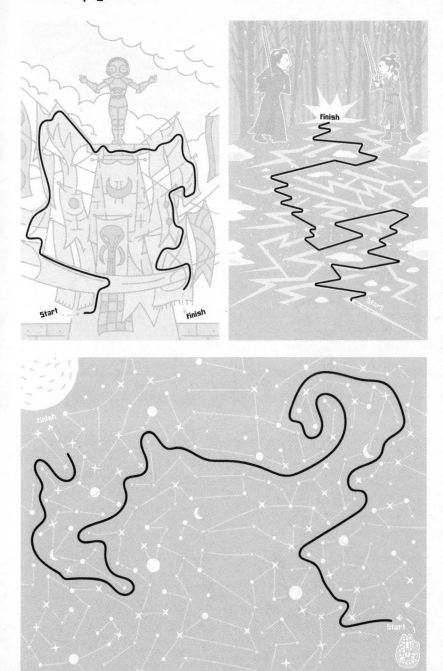

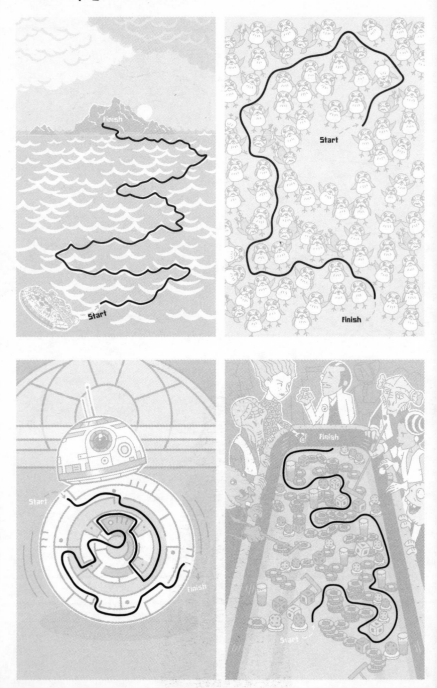

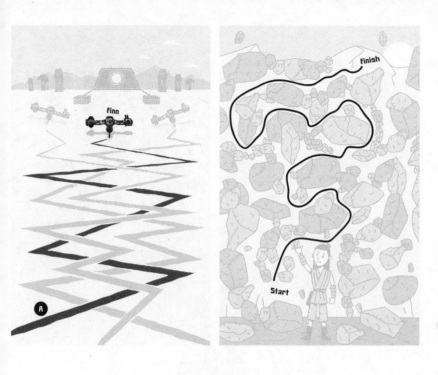